As One Day Slips Out of the Shoe of Another

As One Day Slips Out of the Shoe of Another

Poems by

Marcia J. Pradzinski

Cover design by Shay Culligan

ISBN: 978-1-954353-78-7

Kelsay Books
502 South 1040 East, A-119
American Fork, Utah, 84003
Kelsaybooks.com

for my parents
Julia Seremak and Clemens Pradzinski
and their parents

Acknowledgments

Sincere gratitude to the editors of the following journals and websites where versions of my poems found a home.

Aeolian Harp Anthology Six, Glass Lyre Press: "Caught"
After Hours: "My Father's Last Words to Me," "The Call of Coffee"
Blue Hour Magazine: "Behind Glass," "Memory of Cleaning Fish"
Brevity Poetry Review: "Vespers"
Clementine Unbound: "Kindergarten 1950"
Distilled Lives Anthology: "Material Geography"
East On Central & Your Daily Poem: "on a winter day"
Ekphrastic Review: "Echo"
Exact Change Only: "The Water That Brought Them Here Still Floods Me"
Jo-Anne Hirshfield Award: "Summer's Lament"
JOMP & Jo-Anne Hirshfield Award: "the formica table," "The Scent of Chicken"
Journal of Modern Poetry: "Slipping Back"
Olentangy Review: "Pinned in Place"
Origami Poems Project: "From the Porch," "Language of Absence," "Still Life: Apron"
Pangolin Review: "Kindling"
Paper Swans Press, UK, & Aeolian Harp Anthology Six of Glass Lyre Press: "The Quickening"
Paper Swans Press, UK, Chronicles of Eve: "When I Ask My Father to Sign College-Prep Forms"
Pirene's Fountain, Skin Deep Anthology: "Kitchen Portrait"
Poetica Review: "Father"
RHINO: "All That Moves Her through This World"
Sonic Boom: "Renovation on Walton Street"
Unlost: "Long Evenings," "Study"
Writing in a Woman's Voice: "As If There Is Meaning"

Endless thanks to Patrice Boyer Claeys whose careful readings, keen eye, and perceptive feedback helped me urge this manuscript to life. Sincere gratitude to Plumb Line Poets for their inspiration and encouragement. Deeply grateful to my husband Patrick Quigley who has supported all my poetic endeavors.

Contents

I

Kindling

In all my days I look for light
between the clouds, among the crowds
near downtown buildings rising high
in moonlit puddles splashing bright
in children's eyes intense at play.

I search and search and search some more
in dew that's settled on the ground
releasing scents of dense moist earth
and childhood memories of a yard
a garden plush like Eden lush

with faces and voices rising
a family gathered round a table
singing praying fighting too—
and at that spot I glimpse a spark
that loss has not extinguished.

So now I settle in to rest
not only seeking outside light
I also bask in radiance
and beams of times now past
that linger in my memory's cradle.

Grandma Reflects on Events Leading to Her Marriage in the 1870s

I shivered and tears flooded my face
as my brother Pavel and I huddled together
in steerage. I was nine. Pavel just turned twelve.
We were sent on our way to America
for a good education, Tato said. After Mamo died,
he would talk all the time about the jobs, the schools,
the wealthy who paved sidewalks with gold flowing
toward their children in waves. We didn't care.
We didn't want to go there without him. He said
he would follow once we were set up
with our uncles in Chicago.
He never did.

I thought we were safe until Pavel got lost,
and my uncles didn't try very hard to find him.
My uncles did not take care of us like they told
Tato they would. They sent me to work
at a cigar factory where I earned nine cents a day.
And with that, I paid them rent.

Yes, oh yes, I got a good education!
The small cigar box where I liked to hide
some pennies for candy often stood empty
after a drunken uncle roughed me up
and raided my room. So at 16, I learned to fly,
and got caught in a different cage.

Long Evenings

Water

rose

beside   the   coast

where
emigrants set down

at the start of

waiting for   waiting

Echo

. . . there is no break between the two substances and no limit.
—Rene Magritte

Magritte's woman stares as if in a trance—
black hair, red lips, oval face, black almond eyes
held still. Wood-grain strands swim onto her right hip,
her midriff, and higher to striate her breast. Mahogany
grain swirls onto her right arm, up the hill of her shoulder,
then drops to engrave her left forearm. Seductive fingers
sliver forward to impregnate her. They graze
her lower lip, evoke a shadowy smile.

*

I imagine my grandfather, a cabinetmaker,
chiseling design and shape onto slabs
of wood. Lost in its fragrance, its pliant spirit,
he hums as his tools work their magic. The wood
guides his leathery hands the way stone leads
a sculptor's. He engraves patterns onto edges
of a table, the wood feeding through fingers
no longer his own.

The Water That Brought Them Here
Still Floods Me

Lakes, rivers, oceans fight
to reach me. Their stories surge
in moonlit waves…

a quicksilver flash of my grandparents
who lost children to disease as they gasped
in the drowning eddies of English…

my father's work apron, stiff with oil
from his days as a machinist,
hung idle on mornings spent fishing for perch…

my mother's stern face melted into smiles
as she watched her grandchildren laugh
and splash in the backyard wading pool…

Lakes, rivers, oceans fight
to reach me. Their stories surge
in moonlit waves as I try to pull them to me.

II

From the Porch Window

Lilacs perfume the air. Pruning shears open close open close. Twigs and blossoms sprig my father's flannel shirt. He sets down the clippers and moves to the roses. He bends, slips his fingers under a bright yellow head, and inhales deeply. Sharp sunlight and ginger leaves gild the ground, cast him in an aureole; the shimmer holds him still.

When I Ask My Father to Sign College-Prep Forms

He lights his *Camel* and stands up
from his easy chair to face me.

His shoulders
forward and down

as he taps the *Camel*
over the ash tray. The cigarette,

a teacher's wooden pointer—
"You're just a machinist's daughter."

Smoke curls the air,
dissolves his face.

Memory of Cleaning Perch

my father scrapes
scales from the fish
we caught

his callused hand cups
the shimmer of skin
finds the ruby-bead
button of the belly
the knife splits
open

what filled the body
slips
to cold white porcelain

stained
the knife alone remains

Still Life: Apron

In the basement
across from a wooden
handmade work bench
a machinist's apron hangs
from a metal hook on the wall.
Oil soaks the canvas cloth,
weighs it down
makes it look darker and older
than it is.

Two pockets pouch open
like twin mouths tired
and waiting for food.
A bamboo fishing pole
leans on the wall next to the apron
with a promise of rest, of a wash
of waves infusing the air,
of lake water fragrances loosing
tight muscles—

rest with the promise of food
for hungry mouths.

Cloud Burst

my eyes track thick
brooding bundles

               the sting
               my father's slap
               when I was 12
               You question my judgment?
               my anger stored in an attic
               of hurts

clouds
taut in cumulous coils
wait for a clap of thunder
               lightning

               my father baits a hook
               after throwing back
               the baby perch I caught to
               let it grow up

a robin on rain-softened ground
a worm looped in its beak
sparks a slow release

clouds let go

Slipping Back

As I make my way—

I see peonies
bursting bright pink,
heads surrendering
to the ground,
dark and moist
with evening rain
that slaked the grass
along the way
and left puddles
of tinsellated sunlight
that warms me

to fragrant lilacs
shivering the air
in the front yard
of a house
not far away
calling me back
to the lilac bush
on Walton Street
and the backyard
of yellow tea roses,
tiger lilies, and tulips
primped and pampered
by my father's hands until—

my hand opens the door of Duxler Auto.

My Father's Last Words to Me

Tubes snake from holes
in his arms.
Restraints hold
his parchment hands still
on sheets, bleached white.
At the sides of the bed
metal contraptions grow
an odd jungle
glistening
in sunlight, unrelenting.

He wants to talk
but words stumble
away from him.
Shaking his head,
he says,

"There's nothing
you can do about it,"
he stops
to weigh his final words:

"That's the way,

         the base
  ball."

When I leave, a cool wind rushes over me, clears away
odors of antiseptic and urine. As I make my way to the bus stop,
tears loosen at the tattoo of a pneumatic drill breaking concrete.

Father,

I was scrambling eggs
while you were dying

you floated away
in a fog I try to penetrate

I see only
splinters of your life

you roll corn silk cigarettes

your belt-waving mother chases you in the prairie

you work for years as a house painter

you tickle my fingers on a sunny Sunday morning

         even in
      sleep I can't let go

  you squeeze my hand at the lakefront on a Sunday afternoon

   your sweat mingles with the paint in stranger's houses

    your mother searches for you among the
        prairie cattails

   you smoke corn silk rolled in newspaper strips

splinters are all I have left
after you faded

into a fog
while I was scrambling eggs

summer's lament

the day warms
but I want
my rust-brown sweater
lined tweed pants
bulky knit cap

I want a steamy
breath of tea
a hearty stew
a book
to bury myself
from knowing

I can never
touch him
again

Language of Absence

The Chicago A-frame on Walton Street where I grew up still stands, but the umbrella-shaped mulberry tree and henna-hued lilies no longer grace the front yard. A metal sculpture, shaped like a lily's pointed petals, reaching for air, stands in its place.

I can still see my father plant and water in the backyard every day in spring, summer, and fall—the smell of moist earth, a dog barking; the lilac bush flowering near the alley; the heady scent of lilacs, roses, and mint. Mint, the one plant that annoys my dad because it shoots up everywhere! An abundance of wild, rust-colored tiger lilies edges the back porch—petals speckled reddish-brown like my mother's freckles and auburn hair.

I walk along a block in Skokie. Red-gold daylilies sprout at the corner of a front yard lot. They graze my arm and remind me of the purple morning glories twining in and out of the neighbor's cyclone fence on Walton Street.

III

mother and child

—in response to *Compassion Moves a World,*
sculpture by *Julie Rotblatt-Amrany*

her arms stilled in bronze
anchor and bracelet the boy
in a sunlit hug

his legs cradle her waist
fear fixed in his eyes gentles
as the bowl of her lap
secures him

his feet reach to a metal ribbon
flowing from mother and child
to the globe they stand on

with hope
to grace the world beyond
their bronzed bodies

kitchen portrait

my mother's hands
powder the wheat-hued
breadboard and smooth
flour evenly

her wedding band
a part of her body
glints gold
on the puffy flesh
of her ring finger

she rests the dough ball
on her palm and
rolls it from right
hand to left as her fingers
pat its round bloom

the dough something
she can prompt
with a tender whisper
into the shape
she fashions

her floured arms lean
into the compliant mass
palms massaging
its growth

snowy dots freckle
her arms and she pushes
hard as the windows
darken around her

Material Geography

I watch the outline of a dress begin to form
as my mother feeds the fabric's landscape

to the needle point. The machine's purring softens
the air in the room.

The plat of cotton takes shape, an island
rising from her hands that stream the cloth forward

into a circle of stitches to create armholes.
She holds up the garment to admire her handiwork

and shows me the Communion dress she's sewing for me.
Why do you still have to make my clothes? I stamp my foot.

Why can't I get my dress at Finkelstein's like the other girls?
Cotton, corduroy, wool, silk comfort my mother now.

She leans on her Bernina, swims her hands along lengths
of fabric that wait for her fingers to map

undiscovered landscapes as I slowly drift away.

Renovation on Walton Street

1

Green wallpaper comes down in strips, green not as light as mint or as dark as the avocado stove and fridge in the kitchen. Green replaced a dusty rose my mother had tired of. And now I'm tearing down her choice to make way for eggshell white. Each wallpaper tongue puffs out dust that floats on my hands, arms, hair, and ladder; I peel, uncover plugs of plaster stuck to the paper, and release more than worn-out wallpaper.

2

When I was in grade school I wanted to change my mother, strip her clean, trade in her plump body for one like the younger, slimmer mothers I saw at school, take her out of her sensible shoes, put her in stilettos. I wanted to renovate her, modernize her, rebuild her. Why did she have to sew her own clothes as well as my sisters' and mine, go to millinery school to learn to make hats for the four of us, insist that I learn to sew, and drag me to church with her on Friday evenings when all I wanted was to spend the evening planted in an armchair next to my father, watch the *Cavalcade of Sports* on TV, and hear the singing parrot advertise Gillette blue blades?

3

The history of the Walton Street house appears. Ghosts from my past float, linger, and nudge my working hands.

Behind Glass

in a snapshot on her nightstand
lace collar
flatters a face dappled with freckles
eyes cinnamon-warmed
lips pursed
the budding bush
in the photo fills the room
with fragrance of her youth
blossoming to lilacs

   a sepia fossil
      gilt-framed
         frozen under glass

now
she stares out the window
waiting for someone
to tell her
why she is waiting

As If There Is Meaning

The hospital elevator dings and delivers me
to ICU, to my mother stroked comatose

I step into her room   my legs hesitant   heavy

as if
her dying body weighs them down
and she doesn't want me to see her
motionless   drained of energy

the very energy that fueled her hours ago
to bake a batch of blueberry muffins

as if
she knew her family would need nourishment
after seeing her body   lying stone-still

I walk to her bedside to fix
the crumpled sheet

my fingers skim the back of her feet
her toes reflex up and down

as if
to say
good-bye

study

                  Lonely night

                               stars

hanging down

                emptiness

    the moon

                    like some spook bird

                solo

and roped

        between

           rotting   and   sky

Revenant

                                        that you seem to be

              the eyes
of a child

              a woodpecker
                        pound
              pound
                              pounding
                    on
              our elm tree

a stranger's
              flaming red
                        hair

                                        is true
                                            is not   true

                    your body's cells
              left here
                        free
fall
        float

                              pulse
              survive

                        through breath
        of air
                        the breeze

touching
        transforming
                        other bodies

Ode to a Coffee-Stained Mug

Its thin brown belt reminds me
how my mother's cinnamon-flecked
eyes sparkled when she laughed.
How she and I chatted, two adults
at the Formica table. How,
when I was a child, she fingered
my hair to relax me. I imagine
her warm, freckled hand grazing mine
as she lifts the mug to her lips.
I can't imagine how the shape
was stained into the bottom
of the cup, but I believe my mother
was somehow responsible for it—
a heart, inked in coffee, perfectly formed.

All That Moves Her Through This World

The memory of a memory of a remembered
moon moving in the upper window
or in the face of a beautiful child—
a front in the weather of the room,

just one different thing. It leads us to a ledge and pushes us over
to her absence and holds her.
Her song is the door back to the room
to another, like the shadow of smoke rising.

The slabs of sidewalk pushed up like crooked teeth by what grew
underneath,
dressing, undressing the fabulous wounds.
House her in the coil of my hair,
where finally we meet to touch and sleep.

Day slides by

as the sun makes room
for the moon.

I fall into a daze
that shrouds losses
deeper
than my misplaced keys
or coffee cup...until...

a train howls past a sturdy brick façade.
Its back lot, vacant and vast
in icy moonlight,
lays bare
a wellspring of tears.

IV

Mom Sends Me to the Corner Store Alone

not knowing why the glass door I pass by makes me look wiggly
not knowing why my stomach feels wormy when I see the door

knowing Mommy cupped a quarter into my hand with her fingers
knowing I have to ask for 25 cents of football sausage

not knowing how to count change
not knowing if the cash register lady will give me a tootsie roll

knowing I will gobble a piece of the lunch meat before I get home
knowing Mommy says she's giving me *big-girl responsibility*

not knowing how to read street signs
not knowing why I don't have a brother or sister to walk with me

knowing I have to look both ways when I cross the street
knowing my address is 8 5 2 Hoyne Avenue

not knowing if the door will wiggle me if I run real real fast
not knowing why ants jump inside me when the door sees me

Caught

At five years old in a fabric store I shoplifted
four shades of thread—cardinal, canary,
angel wings, and nun's habit.
Mother, a seamstress, had an order
to fulfill and no cash for those colors.

I hid them in my coat. Four small spools—
a gift for my mother. When she saw my pockets
bulging like a squirrel's nut-filled cheeks, her eyes
narrowed, her lips pursed. Pointing at my stash
she hissed, *You put that back. Right now!*

That night the moon peeked in my bedroom window—
a luminous icicle pointing…pointing…pointing…

Kindergarten 1950

black rosary beads *click-clack*
patrol the rows of wooden tables
Tuesday's air raid siren screams

boys separate from the girls
the nun quick-steps to an elbow-poking boy
black rosary beads *click-clack*

mimeographed nativity scenes
mix with the smell of waxy crayons
Tuesday's air raid siren blares

the nun clutches her rosary beads
her eyebrows bunch and bristle
black rosary beads *click-clack*

she marches to my chair
drags it out scraping the floor
Tuesday's air raid siren shrieks

you're not a baby she yells
yanks my thumb from my mouth
black rosary beads *click-clack*
Tuesday's air raid siren screams

My Mother Thinks I'm Too Young to Share Her World

The round Earth of dough settles its weight
on the wheat-hued bread board. I smell
the future in it—sweet yeasty curls intoxicate
the kitchen space with warmth before the birth
of a full-grown bread waiting for butter,
impatient hands, tongues, teeth.

My mother's palms push and flatten
the Earth as if denying the truth of its shape.
I, too, want to touch and knead and feel
the force of a world rising from my hands.

the Formica table

flashes quicksilver
     in sunlight
          under a bare bulb

dresses for dinners in oilcloth
of apples   pears   bananas
   floating on a beige drop of sky

holds bowls of chicken soup teeming
with diced carrots onions
     and parsnip taken for potato
          and gagged on by the six-year-old

bears steaming plates of pot roast
     stuffed cabbage
          fried chicken   beef stew

amid the heady
     brew of coffee the clank of silverware
       and chatter at the table

the heft of the past rises
     from the scratched face and rusted legs
         that now stand still in a corner of the attic

The Call of Coffee

You seduced me for so long with your exotic,
steamy curls that scented our family kitchen.

You filled my mother's cup and warmed her hands,
cleared the morning haze that masked her day's routine.

My sister chewed your glossy brown-black beans
and tongued the lusty richness of your body.

My sisters and brothers all old enough to take part
in the sacred ritual of coffee, but I was not. My mother

forbade you to enter my body, titillate my palate.
Children should not drink coffee, her mantra. So I waited

for my time to take you in. I stood in Bankes' coffee store
on Chicago Avenue enveloped in your heady perfume

as my mother chose fresh beans. I rubbed my palm and
the back of my hand on the thick, burlap bags where you rested—

the rough texture so different from the silkiness I felt when,
against my mother's warnings, I slipped my hand into the open

mouth of a burlap bag and inhaled deeply. Fingering the beans,
I heard the call of your rustling whisper. Tired of waiting my turn,

I told my mother, *Janet drinks coffee, and she's my age.*
When my mother nodded with pursed lips, my aunt offered me

a flowered cup filled with coffee. My heart beat fast as I waited
for the taste to match your intoxicating fragrance,

but your bitterness stung my tongue, and broke my heart.

Pinned in Place

Sometimes I wish I were still out on the front stoop
with my friends, the house's A-frame pointing us
to the stars while we sip from pink cans of Tab
that shoot us into effervescent dreams, our hands
moist from the cans bleeding summer sweat.

We count fireflies dotting the brick three-flats
across the street, pretend they flash light
on the lives inside. Our hearts race with revving
motors that purple the air with heady fumes.

We gossip about kissing in the schoolyard at night,
lipstick shades, mascara, and stilettos. We whisper
about boys so our mothers won't hear.
We want to fly wild into the drag-racing night.

V

on a winter day

bark tendrils
        gasping for light
           sprig the air
    roost

and wait
    for the impulse
        for the sap   to synapse
                into a burst
      of green buds

The Quickening

Inside this house I lie in a room that rustles
with a stir of light and dark. A natural childbirth
book rests on the floor. I gaze up at the high
ceilings and unpainted walls, see myself
as a fetus, curled in the womb of this house
where I grew up, where ghosts now roam.

Inside this room an upright piano stands.
I doze, float timeless to a permeable past—
Moonlight Sonata echoes in a daydream
that awakens the room's past lives.

Inside this dream I drift downstairs
to the concrete-floor basement. There,
the coal bin where I had imagined
the devil festering. There, inside
a closet my mother's cut patterns
lie boxed, waiting for her hands.

Inside me, a quivering stirs—a butterfly
broken free of a chrysalis testing new-
sprouted wings. I place my hand
on my abdomen as the house cocoons us.

The Scent of Chicken

I watch my father bone perch at the dinner table:
He edges a table knife between the flesh and spine

lifts the body away from the skeleton
and pulls up the frail ladder of bones

that gave shape and structure to the fish.
A ladder of years separates me from my parents,

but they stream back to me in the scent of alewives
on the lake shore sands

where my father holds my hand
on long Sunday afternoon strolls

or in the heady fragrance of duck blood soup simmering
and baked bread waiting

for a slathering of butter spread by my mother's knife
and a chat at the kitchen table.

Even in childbirth, my belly splayed open
to deliver my son

the ghost of a memory rises:
I imagine the scent of chicken

but am told *no cafeteria near here* by the nurse
as he continues to stitch and clean me.

Only weeks later when I visit a live poultry shop
where I went with my mother does the smell convince me

my mother was there
at the birth of her grandson.

Vespers

—after Nancy Willard

When the last shadow falls out of the day
and the sun turns into the moon
and the vestments above become constellations
nothing is gone but the noise
        crowds carry away in their trucks
        children dream of in their sleep
        and mothers silence with their whispers

When dusk dreams of the sun
as it drifts into sleep
the present becomes the past,
and one day slips out of the shoe of another.

Erasure Sources

"Long Evenings" Erasure of Eavan Boland's "The Long Evenings of Their Leavetakings"

"Study" Erasure of Rickey Laurentiis's "Study in Black"

Cento Sources

"All That Moves Her through This World"
Reginald Dwayne Bells, Lawrence Joseph, Billy Collins, Peter Cooley, Robert Gibb, Elaine Equi, Fady Joudah, Joy Katz, Maxine Kumin, Marie Howe, Noelle Kocot, Honor Moore, Jenny Johnson

About the Author

Marcia J. Pradzinski, a retired ESL instructor who taught university and university-bound students, is the author of *Left Behind,* a chapbook published by *Finishing Line Press* in 2015. She was born and raised in a Chicago neighborhood, now dubbed The Ukrainian Village. Her family didn't travel much, but hearing a variety of languages—Polish, Ukrainian, and Spanish—enriched her childhood. She has served as a poetry judge for the Society of Midland Authors and is an active board member of Poets & Patrons of Chicago. Her poems have appeared or are forthcoming in *RHINO, Pirene's Fountain, Paper Swans Press*-UK, *Mom Egg Review, SWWIM, After Hours, Aeolian Harp Anthology Six, Writing in a Woman's Voice,* and *Poetica Review* among others. Her poetry has received awards from *Journal of Modern Poetry, Jo-Anne Hirshfield Memorial Contests,* Highland Park *Poetry Challenges,* and *Pen2Paper.*

www.ingramcontent.com/pod-product-compliance
Lightning Source LLC
Chambersburg PA
CBHW031152090426
42738CB00008B/1292